# WHAT'S WHAT

# WHAT'S WHAT

## Julie O'Callaghan

## BLOODAXE BOOKS

ISBN: 1 85224 161 6

First published 1991 by
Bloodaxe Books Ltd,
P.O. Box 1SN,
Newcastle upon Tyne NE99 1SN.

Bloodaxe Books Ltd acknowledges
the financial assistance of Northern Arts.

Cover reproduction by V & H Reprographics, Newcastle upon Tyne.

Cover printing by Index Print, Newcastle upon Tyne.

Printed in Great Britain by
Bell & Bain Limited, Glasgow, Scotland.

*For my parents*

# Acknowledgements

Acknowledgements are due to the following, where some of these poems were first published or broadcast: *Encounter, The Honest Ulsterman, The Irish Times, Krino, New Statesman, The Observer, Orbis, Oxford Poetry, Poetry Canada Review, Poetry Ireland Review, Poetry Review,* RTE Radio and Television, *The Steeple, The Sunday Tribune, The Times Literary Supplement,* Trinity Closet Press. 'Well-Heeled' appeared in a limited edition from Gefn Press, London.

Poems in this book were also included in the following anthologies: *Firebird 4* (Penguin, 1985), *Soho Square* (Bloomsbury, 1989), *Poems for UNICEF* (Dedalus, 1990) and *The New Younger Irish Poets* (Blackstaff, 1991).

# Contents

# PART I

# In *Betty's of Winnetka*

Judy the sales assistant
is being praised at the moment
by Mrs Chester Finnerman:
'This little lady,' she announces to us,
'knows what's what about clothes.'
She gives Judy a gentle shove
on her left shoulder.
'She has helped me develop
my *entire* wardrobe.
She tells ya if yer tushy is too enormous
for a pair of pants
like it was outta the mouths of babes.
You guys know how it is
with people saying that kinda stuff –
but not with her. Oh no, she makes it sound
like it was a compliment!'
We stand at the pay desk in awe.
'She and she alone has stopped me
looking like a schmuck like I used ta.'
All of our eyes travel up and down Mrs Finnerman's edifice.
'Chester says it isn't right
that a woman of my years
should look so desirable.'

# Adios

You shoulda seen
what a lump on a log I was.
I was the certified chauffeur
for all the family.
Dolly has piano lessons?
Dad'll drive you.
My wife is goin' to the Jewel Food Store?
Get old drippo to sit behind the wheel.
But it was more than that.
There were these eight people
all grabbing my dough
on a Friday night;
eight mouths waiting for Hamburger Helper,
and after I'd bought them
their Dream Whip
and their Keds gym shoes
they start calling me a square.
I was corny they said.
My daughter called me a male chauvinist pig
cuz I was enjoying the half-time entertainment
with the Dallas Cowboys' cheerleaders
kicking up their heels.
This is a gyp, I told myself.
I can't even relax
during a crummy football game.
I got my car keys
and headed for sunny Florida.
So long chumps.

# Content and Tasteful

Here I am in my kitchen.
I look content and tasteful.
When my darling grandchildren
visit their grandma, I give them
windmill cookies – the ones with chunks
of nuts that come wrapped
in the orange cellophane package
with scenes of old Holland.
In this oven I cook up a storm.
Ya gotta garnish your recipes.
Cut out pictures from magazines
like *McCall's* or *Family Circle*
and always make your dishes
look like in the photographs.
I keep a few tricks up my sleeve
in these cabinets only I don't tell them
to anybody except my daughter
in Sarasota Florida who's trying
to get to a man's heart
through his stomach.
That's the only exception.
Do you get the aroma of my
Devil's Food Cake baking?
Ladies, don't waste your time
with most of these new appliances.
Get your basics, keep 'em clean, buy fresh,
and I guarantee you your mouth
will be watering and your girdle
will be killing you.

# Well-Heeled


So what's to live for?
I'm placing a Gold American Express card
on the cash desk – seven hundred and fifty dollars
down the drain
for a fantasy rhinestone pump
with spike heels.
Yesterday, it was paisley-gilded
black brocade lace-ups with a louis heel.
My analyst said, 'Indulge.'
So I'm indulging already!
I think I'd rather have an affair.
My grecian slave sandals
would come in handy for that
or maybe my fuchsia satin court shoes
depending on the man.

I started my girls off right.
As soon as they put a foot on terra firma
I got them little Edwardian slippers:
pink sides with a white toe and bow.
I can still see them teetering along
with frilly cotton socks and Easter bonnets.
I have those shoes up in the attic someplace.
I wonder which box they're in...

Nobody gives a damn about shoes anymore.
Will Sammy the Hong Kong mailman
want to seduce me in my red-rabbit-fur bedroom slippers?
Who's to appreciate – Glen, my spouse?
What a joke!
He trots off in his Gucci loafers to work
and you might as well be wearing
hiking boots under your negligee
for all he cares.
So I head for Neiman-Marcus Shoe Salon –
'the place for women who love shoes'.
If he doesn't notice my fantasy pumps
maybe he'll notice the bill next month
from American Express.

I had a pair of Maud Frizon shoes
that had cute fake watches on the ankle straps.
He kept mocking them by kneeling down in front of me
'to see what time it is'.

*Did you tell that shrink of yours*
*about the Calvin Klein princess pumps*
*ya bought a year ago*
*and have never worn cause you say*
*they're too pretty to wear*
*or your Texan snake and pony skin*
*hand-tooled leather cowboy boots*
*that you wear to the supermarket –*
*did ya tell him that –*
*what does all this mean?*
Glen always toys with the dramatic
rather than the mundane in our relationship.

It was a pair of white patent Mary Janes
that made me the way I am today.
I refused to unfasten the strap
out of its golden buckle.
I wore them to bed, to school,
to play in – I even took a bath
with them on once – they made me happy.
One morning I woke up
and they were gone.
Words cannot convey that catastrophe.

Last week I wore a sea-green
suede-fronded ankle-boot
on my head to a party.
I went barefoot.
Maybe this is a development.

# Big Herms

Mothers of the world
I hope you aren't
in Big Herms Hot Dog Stand
for Mother's Day
like I am.
My girlfriends are out
having lunch
with their happy families
at the Ramada Inn smorgasbord.
'What the heck is this?'
I ask myself.
I look around at the clientele:
thugs, Hell's Angels, creepos.
Herm gave me a doggy bag
with the remains
of my Mother's Day Special.
I drove out to a neighbourhood
where I'm anonymous,
ate my dog and slaw.
My kids live out on the coast.
Their mother and her humiliation
might as well be mustard
at the bottom of the bag.

# Change

Are you a woman
between the ages of 49 and 51?
I bet you feel like
elbowing the person
beside you at the cucumber display
or making mean faces
at somebody
you don't even know
on your way to work
each morning.
Do you say nasty things
about the couple across the street
and want to belt those kids
making so much noise?
I can sympathise.
Only, ladies, stop it.
That's a bad way to act.
Get a grip on your bio-rhythms.
Hormone Replacement Therapy
can have dramatic results.
Why not ask your doctor about it today?

## Year-at-a-Glance

All of you go-getters out there
who publish *Fire Safety Monthly*
and *Metal Trade Weekly*
or *Soap, Perfume and Cosmetics International*
or *Chemical Compounds*
quit putting those
ugly old year-at-a-glance
wall calendars in your magazines
every December
as if you're doing us
this big favour.
Why not have a pow-wow next time
and opt for a sun visor with logo
or a washable pocket pen organiser?
Something handy
and covetable
instead of graphically illustrating
a year full of empty boxes.

# Humming

Such a meshuganah!
Getting married in an empty office space,
without an organ, what schmaltz!
Every place you look – Mexicans – swarms of 'em.
Reminds me of *West Side Story* for godsake.
Come to gawk as a hot tamale lassos a gringo –
a Jewish gringo – into walking down the aisle
(I mean hallway).
So what does the Rabbi tell us to do?
'Please commence humming the Wedding March
as I'd like to get this show on the road.'
The Jewish contingent hums.
The Mexicans don't understand at first,
but when the office door opens,
and the bride trots in, they catch on
and hum along – such humiliation!
I should have brought my harmonica...
I'm looking around and shaking my head:
You call this a melting pot?
It's more like a pressure-cooker.
And this genius of a kid – it makes me weep –
ten years of Hebrew lessons down the drain;
not to mention that Bar Mitzvah,
must've set his dad back a few grand...
Then we had a little more humming,
threw some confetti, took a few snaps –
good thing I brought my Swiss Army Knife;
that's in case of any shenanigans
at the taco reception.

# Naturally the Foundation Will Not Bear My Expenses

If I were up on 'The Logic of Monsters'
or could cogitate a little bit
on 'The Romantic Suburb in Britain
and America Before 1870'
or 'Aristocratic Friendship
in Early Modern France' or knew
'The Meaning of the Confederate Experience'
I'd be worth at least twenty thou
at the moment.
Instead of zilch.
All I'd have to do is produce some of the old crapola:
'The Uses of Failure and Adversity
in the Culture of Success'
and 'The Causes and Consequences of the
Increasing Concern with Body Image'
and I'd have money in the bank.
Such eggheads!
They are wise on 'The Career of Ch'en Hung-mou
and Statecraft in 18th Century China'
and 'Truth-Telling and the Affections in Poetry'.
They have even made a breakthrough
in a study entitled 'Phrenology
and the Poetical Character'.
Now I see them grabbing their cash and sneering,
'If you're so smart why ain't you dot, dot, dot?'

## Germs on the Phone

You wouldn't believe
how many germs
you clowns have.
You are crawling
with lethal micro-organisms.
How can a guy
protect himself
from these mutant viruses
I frequently ask myself.
That's why I carry
a supply of plastic bags
with me at all times.
If I *must* use
a public telephone booth
I wrap the receiver
in a bag
before holding it to my head.
I run to the nearest garbage can
when I'm done
and dispose of all
your filthy cooties.

## Slow Talking

I'll tell ya:
if you put a box of popsicles
in your grocery cart
and ran into Bea
from two doors down
in front of the
Betty Crocker cake mixes
in White Hen Pantry
the reality is that you have
bought yourself a box of
purple sugar water by the time
you hand over your money
to Shelly at the check-out,
since people in this burg
enjoy talking real slow
and exercising their jaws
and eyebrows for dramatic effect.
'Say Bea, do you have that
recipe for potato chip dip
I went loopy over the
night before last at your house?'
There is no need to rush,
they aren't in life's fast lane,
popsicles or no popsicles.

## Frost and Parties

Eight o'clock with the sun rising
at Howard el station,
tears are freezing on my cheek
and my lips are numb.
Five hours ago I was surrounded
by party-animals belting out
'The Egg-Plant that Ate Chicago'
in mega-decibels wearing paper hats.
The terrain resembled a Die-In
we had once at University –
on the count of three you collapse
onto the street to demonstrate the results
of our military war machine.
Crawling over fallen bodies,
I wanted to get to the telescope
so I could see what everyone else
was doing with themselves.
No boat was sailing in the lake
out past the frozen water.
I saw a few yellow cabs gliding over ice
through skyscraper canyons.
No one was walking anywhere.
I saw a man reading a book
in an apartment so far away
that when I took my eye from the lens
all you could see was a lighted room
about thirty storeys up.

Now I'm a commuter
waiting for my train.
I execute a tribal war dance:
stamp foot, stamp foot, swear.
Talman Federal Savings is communicating
to me with teensy moving light bulbs:
'12 below, 10 past 8, BRRRRRRRR!!'

# Pep-Talk to Poets from Their Sales Manager
*(for Gerald Dawe)*


Alright, you Irish guys –
first off – I love ya – got it?
Hey – where's the blarney?
Quit looking like you were just included
in a 'Contemporary British Poetry' anthology
or something; we got books to sell!
Now, what abouta few Volkswagens in bogs
or grey streets with graffiti on the walls –
scenes like that;
you haven't been turning it out lately.
How come? I need stuff with slogans, guys.
Folksy stuff – know what I mean?
I'm doin my best but it's all lookin
a little like a yawner at this stage.
That's all, lads – keep at it.


I wanna see all a you extra-terrestrials
gravitating over here double quick, fellas.
'Take me to yer reader' – right, guys?
Now let's get serious – huh?
Here's your sales chart – up, up, up!
Kinda like a flying saucer discovering
new universes of humanoids who wanna book of poetry.
We're gonna capture new markets, aren't we,
and no more traitors writing
transvestite translations or we'll zap them
with our lazer gun – right?


Goils! Move yer feminist little butts over here.
Yer doin terrific. Lots of sarcasm
about what termites we guys are, lots of PMT,
lots of mothers acting square – magnificent!
My god, you're going great guns, ladies.
OOPS! I mean WOMEN don't I?
We want a lot of hype comin up to Christmas
so those cash registers keep singing.

Just one word of advice: see if you can
Virginia Woolf-up your images a bit
and who knows what we can do?
Sisterhood is powerful!

All miscellaneous misfits, up front please.
Lookit pals, *you* want an easy life,
*I* wanta easy life and *we all* want super-sales,
so why not give up this poetic individuality baloney
and get yourselves an angle, join a group.
My job is tough enough
without you weirdos
lousing it up even more!

# Baha'i Temple, Wilmette, Illinois

Anyone who wants to start tooting a horn
around this neck of the woods
about the Taj Mahal should hold his horses.
No siree – Wilmette, Illinois –
we're not just another run-of-the-mill
hole-in-the-wall suburb.
Got a world atlas, folks?
Why not go and get one right now
so you can see what the hell I'm talking about.
I bet little Junior had it hidden
under his collection of model airplanes – huh?
Can you find the page with Chicago on it?
OK, now we're cooking guys.
Cast your eye to the north a bit
along the shoreline of Lake Michigan
and you'll see Wilmette mentioned
on any respectable map – if not,
sorry pal, but you've bought a hunk of junk.

Now that you know where we're located
on the face of the earth
come on out and visit us.
Boy oh boy are you in for a big surprise
when you realise what's sitting majestically
high atop a hill gazing lakeward eternally.
I'd love to witness your faces
when first setting eyes upon the
Baha'i Temple, Wilmette, Illinois.
See you there!

## Sugar Wedding Rose

Cripes, a little wedding party for my daughter
and because her guy's a Jew
my son's wife walks up to the cake,
grabs a wad of it in her hand
and starts flinging it at the happy couple.
She quits tossing the cake,
grabs the guy's jacket
and divides it straight up the back seam.
Brother, this dame ain't a German for nothing!
Mom starts yellin', 'dial 999, Harry'
and doin' an Irish jig
(my dear wife's brain ain't the best
in her declining years).
I'm not letting coppers into *my* house!
'Hold the phone' I say, 'no keystone cops
are trotting in here for a little
family misunderstanding.'
Whereupon Mom, in her toreador pants,
hops onto the culprit's back hollering,
'STOP WRECKING THEIR CAKE!'
This is just my kind of party, I think,
watching the festivities.
I wipe a sugar wedding rose off the armrest
and pop it into my mouth.

# Wind

Who cares if I am sitting
in this darn old consultant's office
propped up behind my word-processor
and my ultra-modern receptionist desk like a drip
with 48 dollars worth of Estée Lauder creams,
colours and fragrance invested on my being
so that some clown of a manager
can fling himself at me
because he's a mega-client?
'Take a mother's advice,' she kept saying,
'finish your college education
before Mr Right comes along,
or you'll regret it the rest of your life.'
I got a dumb B.A., a 'position of responsibility
in a high-powered, non-stop environment',
I got a bachelorette apartment
in a trendy neighbourhood, I got myself
a Saks Fifth Avenue credit card
and a sports car and so what?
Here I am doing my nails
looking out across Lake Michigan
scattered with teensy sailboats
being blown over by the wind.

# Yuppie Considering Life in Her Loft Apartment

Jeff is such a bastard.
Like I can't handle it.
All I did was throw the silver fork
he'd left stuck for a week
in the mud at the base
of my weeping willow tree
in the general direction of his chest
and while it was en route added,
'What am I, your maid, lunkhead?'
He, as usual, moved *before* the fork
crash landed on his bicep and said,
'No prob, no prob', and those were
his last words to me on his way
out of my orbit and into the
gravitational pull of some dumb broad.
Advice has been pouring in:
'One look and I told you –
he's a no-goodnik, but you said you
liked his shoes, so there's no point
talking to you is there?';
and, 'Cancel him offa yer floppy disk,
revise your memory bank
and write a new programme –
who needs the louse anyway?';
and, 'Join the club. Ya wanna
come with me for a facial? –
Elizabeth Arden have a special offer.'
The part that really gets to me
is that I forgot everything I learned
in that Psychology course I took last year:
'The Male Ego and How to Cope With It'.

# Romance

I am unpacking a box
of sci-fi paperbacks
when somebody not very kosher
catches the corner of my eye.
I cast a glance
in the vicinity of the self-help section
and think to myself,
'That is one helluva tall broad.'
OK, it's a value judgement, I admit it.
Whilst gift-wrapping a Babar-the-elephant book
for a six-year-old, I conjecture:
'The mink alone musta cost around 20 grand!'
All I can see is this six-foot-three,
real-skinny fur-clad back.
So what? Well, as I was saying,
something was rotten in the state of Denmark
about this particular specimen.
I make a mental note of two-inch,
fire-engine-red fingernails
as I'm giving change to a guy
who has just bought some gripping sports books:
*Batty About Baseball* or something like that.
Now she's coming this way and I begin to hum
'Strangers in the Night' in order to keep my cool.
'Would you direct me to the Romance section, love?'
My mouth falls open, my hand is shaking
and my eyes are dancing the tango.
'To the right against the wall.'
'Oh goody, I just love a steamy novel, don't you?'
I nod my silly head
and follow the gold spike heels
sauntering across the carpet.
What *has* happened to the American-macho-man?

# PART II

# OPENING LINES
*Dramaticules*

# Opening Lines

Welcome to Potawotamee Summer Camp.
We ain't interested in any wise-crackers,
smart-alecs, spoil-sports or louses.
Any of the above a-ree-va-dare-chee.
You guys'll be comin wid me for some warm-ups
around the track before we get down to
a few wunnerful games a baseball.
The ladies'll be in da parkhouse for crafts:
keychains, beads and macramé, right Miss Chwingyard?
After lunch we'll all go out to the
volleyball courts for a battle between the sexes.
Losers'll do latrine duty for a week.
Lunch'll consist of
hot dogs with relish, mustard and ketchup, Doritos,
chocolate milk and a piece of cake.
Like it or lump it.

# Auschwitz

I says to him, 'Cutie-pie, come out of that.'
I says, 'You're asking for it, Brad.
These people don't care a damn
if you saved-up for three years
to travel over here – they wouldn't care
if it was ten years and they seem
awful nasty – so I think you'd better
get the hell outta there real soon.'
He kept saying, 'Check the focus;
have you included the whole scene?;
is there enough light?; check it again,
I can't afford another trip if you don't do it right;
can you see my face?'
I took a few snapshots and said,
'You're gonna be murdered if you don't get out
of that rotten old gas oven.'

33

## Federal Case

Wow, I said I'd love a Big Mac
with piles of mush spurting out the sides.
So what? Is it such a Federal Case?
Maybe it's a mortal sin cuz
I've got a yen for some junk food.
You'd have thought I'd cursed his mother
or told him I hated his guts
the way he looked at me
like I was a gun-lobby supporter.
Holy cow, it isn't the end of the world
if some processed, bleached, portion-controlled,
regulated bun and a little cereal-filled meat,
cheese and slop goes plonk into my stomach!
I've gone out with this guy
only five times and already he's getting
like a Nazi over what I want to eat.


## Identification Parade

Pardon me for being so nosy, but aren't you Alexander Solzhenitsyn?
– No, I'm afraid I'm not.
My husband bet me two dollars you weren't.
– So you lose.
Well we didn't shake on it, but I guess I do.
– Better luck next time.
You don't sound Russian, but you are, aren't you?
– I'm from Tipperary, Ireland.
An Irish man – who looks Russian – my god!
– None of my family are Russians either.
Did you ever hear of the un-crowned queen of Ireland?
– As a matter of fact I did.
What was her name again?
– Kitty O'Shea, the mistress of Parnell.
Oh I guess Alexander Solzhenitsyn wouldn't know that.
– Unless he's an Irishman.

## On the Blink

Whatdya keep staring out the window for?
– The TV's on the blink again.
Are you looking for someone to fix it?
– Very funny, Herb, yuk, yuk, yuk.
Ya look dopey sittin there like that.
– Well the scenery in here ain't so gorgeous.
Hells bells, why don't ya jump and get it over with?
– You're a real wise-guy, ya know that?
May I finish the *Sun-Times* now?
– Be my guest, Mr So & So.
I suppose I'm not allowed to ask you anything?
– No I suppose you're not.
What's wrong with you?
– Nothing *you'd* care about.
Then quit displaying yourself to the neighbourhood.
– I can do what I want – it's my birthday.


## Let's Get Physical

Daddy I know lots of neat songs.
– Really? Sing me one.
OK, '*Let's get physical, physical, I wanna get...*'
– Know any others?
Yeah. '*She's a man-eater, watch out boys...*'
– Where'd you learn those?
You play them on the phonograph.
– You've got a good memory for a five-year-old.
'*Lemme hear your body talk, your body talk...*'
– Did you ever sing them for Mommy?
Sure. '*Watch out boys she'll eat you up.*'
– What did she think?
She said I could go with her to the beauty parlor.
– Why d'ya wanna go there?
So nobody'll recognize me after vacation.
– Sing me some more.

## Bed and Breakfast

Um, excuse me an everything
but did you two sleep OK last night?
Ya see neither of us got a wink.
That lady said the bed we'd have
was like a Queen-size and what it really was
was a three-quarter, right Fred?
Fred and me are used to a Queen-size.
We had one ever since our honeymoon.
Can you imagine us in a three-quarter?
Maybe here in Ireland a three-quarter is a Queen-size –
but not in the States, I-can-tell-you!
Gee, we could hardly breathe.
You've gotta really cute country
only Fred and I'd be better off at home
if a three-quarter is a Queen-size.
We'd be too tired to see it.


## Weather

'You shouldn't be outside dressed like that.'
I turn my head toward the voice and smile my
we-have-to-humour-the-loony-element smile.
'Just look at your legs! My gosh, they're scarlet!
You'll get frost-bite, ya know, if you don't
wear something warm on your legs.
Even a little kid'd know that much!'
She rose from the bench, looked down the track,
walked over to the big button on the platform labelled
*Press for Heat*, pressed it and sat down beside me again.
'No mittens, no scarf, nothing on your poor legs,
what do you want to do – end up in a hospital?'
A crowd had formed under the heater.
I edged further away on the bench.
'You'd wanna be nuts to come outside
like that in weather like this.'

## Fancy Dress

My husband and I are heading out soon
for what promises to be a fabulous evening.
I will be attending as a Box Jelly Fish
and my better half is masquerading,
after what I thought was minimum pressure
from me, as a Red Back Spider.
Our brief for costumes had been:
'come as something slimy or creepy',
so we chose one of each – avoiding, of course,
the cliché things like centipedes
and snakes and whatnot. Needless to say,
the first costume we'll see will be a mediocre
serpent of nondescript origins
or an amateurish earwig or maggot.
We've invested a good deal of imagination,
so we hope our efforts will not go unappreciated.


## Matinee

Grandma, whisper, everybody's turning around.
– Well is she being thrown out of the convent?
No, she's just going to be a governess for a while.
– What does she have on?
A brown dress, hat and she's carrying a suitcase.
– Where's she going, is she walking or what?
Yeah, she's walking to the house where she's got the job.
– Why didn't they pick her up in a carriage?
So she could sing a song on the way.
– Is this a true story?
I guess so.
– Well I bet they picked her up.
Now she's meeting the family.
– She marries the father, Ingrid told me.
He's very handsome and rich.
– I thought you said she was still a nun.

## The Ballgame

Mel
– Yeah
Quit watching that baseball game
– Pipe down and get me a Budweiser
Mel
– Whadya want
Let's go see a movie er somethin
– Nah, this next guy might hit a grand slam
Mel
– Go with Shirley er Audrey
I wanna go with my husband
– My god, right the hell outta the ball park
Mel
– Knock it off
I wish WGN would go out of business
– Fat chance blabber mouth


## Slow Puncture

For crying out loud – what is this I see?
– Hey Dad, it's just a flat tire; no big deal.
That is beau–ti–ful, 'just a flat tire' this guy says.
– It must have been a slow puncture.
What, you drove somewhere weird or somethin?
– I'll go change it for christ's sake!
The tow-truck is on its way, Mr Hot-wheels.
– You called a tow-truck for a flat tire?
Ya know how much one of those tires costs?
– Don't exaggerate.
Guess, go on, wise-guy, guess already.
– I'm not playing this game.
Of course you're not playing – you wrecked my tire.
– It's *not* wrecked – I'll change it.
A hundred ninety big ones – I'm not talking peanuts.
– OK – I'll collapse on the floor – alright?

## Getting Nowhere

Do you think I look weird or something?
Maybe I look like Betsy Hogan
and I don't even know it. She's got zits
even on her neck! Or I guess
it could be B.O. or bad breath – which is it?
God, *what* is it? Not one guy has ever
even talked to me, except Joey
in my American History Class
and he doesn't count since he's at least
four inches shorter than me.
It must be pretty drastic whatever it is.
Even Carol Schwartz got asked out last weekend.
Like it's totally unreal. My mom goes,
'You're just a late-bloomer like your Aunt Mitzi'
but I don't buy that.
I just don't have any sex-appeal.


## Off the Rails

It was kinda scary how he was just staring
like a lunatic at the ingredients
on the cornflake box. I kept an eye on him
pretending not to and said, 'Stanley, what's a matter
with you anyhow? Why don't ya eat-up
or you'll miss yer train?'
He just said, 'shut-up' and it wasn't
really like him to say that to me.
'That's a great thing to say to me,
when it's 8:23 and the train goes
at 8:30 exactly and ya still haven't
started breakfast.' He just picked up his spoon
and started tapping his cereal bowl
real slow like a bell.
He stayed up in his room until midnight.
That was just the start of the problem.

# Quiz

Who do you think this is?
– OK, who?
I'm asking *you*! Here's a hint: chicken gai pan.
– I don't know.
Second hint: goochy, goochy, goo.
– I'm hanging up.
Wait, wait, I'm serious – honest.
– Is it my ridiculous cousin Grover?
You're not even trying.
– Is it Herman the milkman?
Third hint: corner of Chicago Avenue and Michigan.
– Do you sell balloons?
Close – you're getting warm!
– Bill, will you quit calling me up?
Not till you come out with me.
– OK, first hint: GET LOST.


# Butinsky

Pardon em moi, I own my own clothes shop
and I just can't help telling people
what I think. Now, the jacket you've got on
is too much coat for you.
Look at the back – you can't handle that much coat
with your figure. Try a size smaller.
See? Didn't I tell ya? A different cut, smaller,
neater – now that's really THE LOOK.
Yeah, I'm buying one myself in grey.
You're more a beige. We're going down to Orlando
and last year it was pretty nippy down there.
A jacket is essential. Fort Lauderdale? No,
I haven't heard what the weather is there.
Yeah, last year neither of us exactly cared
how the weather was – we'd be sloshed by 10 a.m.
and after that – what's the difference?

# Vibes

He looked straight into my eye and said,
'What kind of peanut-brain do you think I am?'
– Tungston got that angry? Why?
I go, 'Tungston, what has got yer dander up?'
Can I have one of these Ritz crackers?
– Sure, go on, tell me for heaven's sake!
He just sat there with sweat on his lip
pounding the steering wheel with his fist.
– Whatdymean? You must've done something
for him to act like that – or did you say something?
No sirreebob. I ate a potato chip and offered him one
and he was saying, 'women, women!'
– Did he take one?
He screamed, 'Lookit cookie, I wasn't born
yesterday or the day before neither.'
Then he said, 'You're giving me very bad energy.'


# Living with Pink

What does it look like in the rear end?
– You have to live with this coat, ya know.
Ma, I know already, do you like it?
– It looks like a Perry Ellis.
I think I'll get it.
– Can you live with glow-in-the-dark pink?
I think it's cool.
– Cool? – you gotta wear this thing.
Is it too long? – I can get it altered.
– Take your hands outta the pockets.
Should I buy it?
– The workmanship is shoddy – look at these threads.
I can cut off the threads.
– For five hundred bucks you shouldn't have to.
I really love it.
– But will it last?

## Brats

Tell Wanda ta shut her trap, Mom.
– What's wrong with humming, knucklebrain?
Mom, will ya tell her?
– I can hum when I want – right, Mom?
Not while I'm watching something, sap.
– Reruns of the *Beverly Hillbillies*?
Mom, tell her or I'll bash her one.
– Your son is threatening me, Mother.
Wait till Dad gets home, smarty pants.
– Oh, I'm *so* scared!
Why won't ya tell her to shut her big dumb mouth?
– Quit bossing Mom around.
No stupid, put a cork in it.
– He called me stupid, Mom.
I'm watching something you goddamn moose.
– Now, Mom, he's swearing.


## Make or Break

Milton and I had come to a state
of mutual nothingness in our relationship.
So as I'm driving the kids to their drama workshop,
I say, 'Caitlin and Chip, I'd like to tell you
about something that has happened between Daddy and myself.
Both of us have found new friends
and we don't want to live together anymore.'
I calculated, as I saw their reactions,
that the analyst bills alone
would bankrupt us, not including the divorce lawyers.
Then little Chip says something real cute:
'Why don't you bring your boyfriend to live in our house
and Daddy can bring Patsy and her dog
and we can all stay together and not have to split up?'
Milt said, 'What the hell, we'll give it a try.'
Now we're just one big happy family!

## Double Vision

It was a bolt of light
from out of the blue heavens:
I looked around me as if
I didn't remember where I was or realise
that the daiquiri ice and liquorice whip
double dip was melting.
I staggered into the street,
mopping up my arm and licking
the side of my sugar cone furiously
while saying to myself over and over:
You, Trudy Hemphill, get up off
yer big butt and make yourself
into an achiever, a high-flyer!
I don't know what came over me.
It was as if having a zany double-dip
jump-started my ambition in life.


## Chewing it Over

Big bucks in restaurants means
ya gotta get yerself a gimmick –
they wanna walk over bridges
to their tables with little waterfalls
beside them and fish swimming in ponds
and they want a little class
like Old Vienna cafés and fancy cakes –
they want a bellyful of atmosphere?
Alright you guys, you're gonna get it.
My brain has been masticating over this
and has finally digested all the facts
and ta-da it has found the answer:
it's a pancake joint where the waitresses wear
curlers, bathrobes, slippers and yawn a lot.
The *Come on Down to the Kitchen* breakfast place.

## Window Display

HEY LADY, DO YOU KNOW WHAT TIME IT IS?
– Stop screaming out the window. Call time.
It costs 25 cents to call time.
– It's hillbilly roaring out the window.
BUDDY, YOUR FLY'S OPEN.
– You're gonna get your head bashed-in someday.
Well I'd like to see him try – he must be 80.
– And you act like you're 6.
EXCUSE ME, MISTER, COULD I BORROW A DOLLAR?
– What did he say to that?
Expletive deleted.
– Too bad the window doesn't fall on your tongue.
HEY KID, YOUR MOTHER WEARS SUEDE UNDERWEAR.
– That's a peculiar hobby, insulting people from 5 storeys up.
BONZO, YEAH YOU, YOU'RE A COCKROACH.
– Maybe I could get a book about it in the library.


## You Two

What's wrong with you two?
You don't have such awful-looking faces.
But there you sit in your dressing-gowns
eating cornflakes like there's no tomorrow.
How did everybody else get married?
Don't tell me to shut my big trap –
I'm your mother and you two aren't exactly
in your first bloom of youth.
Nancy's not much to look at
but she made the most of herself.
I don't think I could even count
the number of special novenas I've said,
not to mention how I'm bankrupt lighting candles.
I'd like to meet my grandchildren
some day, so let's all
pull up our socks around here.

# PART III

# Banana Peel

A Cockney man stands in my kitchen
holding with two fingers
an upside-down empty banana skin.
The tops of his beige p.j.s
are neatly tucked
into the elasticated waistband
of the bottoms.
His imitation-leather slippers
co-ordinate with the dark-brown piping
around the collar,
which further complements
his horn-rim glasses.
The banana skin flaps as he looks frantically
in all directions for the
regulation Marks & Spencer pedal-bin.

# Jasper Yawning

Jasper knows the score
so you can forget it – he is not impressed.
He doesn't care about current events
or the weather – he hangs around
in a woollen blanket
and a lime-green snap-up-the-front number
with embroidered lamb.
He keeps out all brain pollution
with a really radical red and white striped
anti-hogwash baby bonnet,
with optional under-the-chin tie string.
Give yourself a break
and dispense with piggys going to market
and goochy-goochy-goos:
this guy hates to see an adult
making an idiot of himself.
His ear-flaps automatically
intercept all baby talk.
He's waiting for his face to grow bigger
because right now
when people take his photograph
or pat him on the back
to make him burp
or tickle him under his arm
or tell him how cute he is
the scope of his yawn is limited –
his eyes and nose keep getting in the way.
But hey, that's just technical –
you're either born a boredom detector
or you ain't, end of story.
I'll zip my lip –
his mouth is starting to quiver.

## Mom and Dad's Bedroom

It has a lived-in look.
A coffee mug is covered
with a Commonwealth Edison bill
which itself is partly obscured
by a pearl necklace and *Health* magazine.
No perfectionist sleeps here –
a shirt balances on its head
in the corner beside tights
that have gone flabby on the floor.
Keys hang from a pegboard.
A note speared to the door with a fork reminds:
'Fill in every check stub.'
Every millimetre of living-space is filled in;
an oriental carpet is decorated with
a cake plate, a letter from California,
an Aran sweater, a psychedelic kite,
a popped button, an umbrella-hat,
an L.L. Bean catalogue, a vitamin catalogue,
a bicycle brochure and a *New York Times*
Travel Section turned to 'What's doing in Antwerp'.
My Mom and Dad are watching TV
over the tops of their toes.
Three aerials scour the void
for signals from downtown Chicago.
Instead of a dial to change channels,
an enormous spoon protrudes from the control panel
with a big tie-up boot balanced by its shoelaces
on the handle
for a more realistic picture.

## What We Talk About

About so and so and whatchacallit
being such louses
or else about what the hell
does this pea brain think he's doing.
Sometimes we discuss topics
to discuss on a BIG DATE,
but first we chew over the gear
the hair the accessories the war paint.
Don't say chew or we'll blab
about craving pineapple upside down cake
and the pig-out last week at Jennifer's.
When someone comes into the office
we've got the ugly skirt cheap blouse
clashing sweater bad skin
corny hair-do and she's awful fond of herself
to mull over for a while.
Then it's back to how crummy the weather is
should we book a sun-bed
the clothes dilemma: to put a deposit
or not to put a deposit
the length of the day
the temperature of the room
the cost of hand cream.
The boss says quit talking –
which will come in handy
as the main topic at break-time.

C

# Managing the Common Herd:
*two approaches for senior management*


THEORY X: People are naturally lazy.
They come late, leave early, feign illness.
When they sit at their desks
it's ten to one they're yakking to colleagues
on the subject of who qualifies as a gorgeous hunk.
They're coating their lips and nails with slop,
a magazine open to 'What your nails say about you'
or 'Ten exercises to keep your bottom in top form'
under this year's annual report.
These people need punishment;
they require stern warnings
and threats – don't be a coward,
don't be intimidated by a batting eyelash.
Stand firm: a few tears, a Mars Bar,
several glasses of cider with her pals tonight
and you'll be just the same old
rat-bag, mealy-mouthed, small-minded tyrant
you were before you docked her
fifteen minutes pay for insubordination.

*Never let these con-artists get the better of you.*

THEORY Z: Staff need encouragement.
Give them a little responsibility
and watch their eager faces lighting up.
Let them know their input is important.
Be democratic – allow all of them
their two cents worth of gripes.
(Don't forget this is the Dr Spock generation.)
If eight out of twelve of them
prefer green garbage cans to black ones
under their desks, be generous –
the dividends in productivity
will be reaped with compound interest.
Offer incentives, show them
it's to their *own* advantage to meet targets.
Don't talk down to your employees.

Make staff believe that they
have valid and innovative ideas
and that not only are you interested,
but that you will act upon them.

*Remember, they're human too.*

## Places, Everyone

Our hero strolls into his office.
He is late.
His red-faced boss follows him
and makes sarcastic remarks:
'It was good of you to grace us
with your presence –
we aren't inconveniencing you – are we?'
The hero smiles hugely, turns,
and with a mighty swipe
rids his desk of invoices, orders,
telephones, blotters, paper trays,
executive toy and name-plaque.
He retrieves his Chicago Cubs Baseball Cap
and, without a word, retires.
That's the showbiz version.
The version on Monroe Street
is a smidgen more pedestrian.
If we take the scene up from 'are we?',
Joe Employee sits down at his desk,
humbly checks his appointment diary,
sees three clients, dictates nine letters,
attends a strategy meeting,
and hopes his misdemeanour
doesn't ruin his chances of promotion.
Repeat this sentence for forty years.

# The Season To Be Jolly

## I. *A Blizzard on Judson Avenue*

A family in eskimo coats waddles past on snowshoes
and a black poodle wearing a tartan ensemble
tiptoes by with red boots.
Two girls in striped hats
struggle through the powdery drifts
with their tongues out, trying to catch a snowflake.
A young executive, with a Christmas tree trunk
at his neck, groans and leaves a mark
like the dragging tail of a peacock.
I open the crystal window and listen for life.
There is no sound anywhere
except the scraping of a sled
piled with grocery bags
gliding down the middle of the street.
By morning, wind and snow
will have repaired the damage.

## II. *Woman Going to Christmas Party*

Now that the babysitter's here,
and the kids in their p.j.s
are hypnotised by Snoopy's Christmas Show,
I can take my hair-rollers out
and put some glitter on my eyelids.
Unfortunately, my youngest puked
on the shoulder of my party-dress,
so I've borrowed a sequined shawl
from next-door and added extra perfume.
Beside the phone, I've left a list
of dos-and-don'ts and a number where,
if all else fails, I can be reached.
Chuck is outside warming up the engine;
but now for the fun part:
digging the car out of a snow-drift.

III. *Santa*

Sometime around Thanksgiving
the missus goes all mush-mash on me
and I can tell stormy weather's ahead.
'Oh Herb-honey,' she says in her
I-just-spent-a-million-dollars-on-a-dress voice,
'the ladies of the Evanston Woman's Club
have given you the supreme honour
of voting you this year's Santa Claus.'
I quit chewing a mouthful of apple pie,
drop (simultaneously) paper, fork, lower jaw
and reply, 'Huh?' as my left hand
clutches my forehead for effect.
So here I sit, with Lester Pugh casting a cynical eye
at my Mr Nice-Guy act as he says,
'Mr Nelson, you ain't Santa Claus.
My mom said we could go and see Santa
and you're just the guy from across the street!'
'Ho, ho, ho, little boy,' I retort, 'Santa only brings
Star Wars spaceships to *good* children.'
'I'll be good, Santa,' says Lester, sprouting horns.


IV. *Snow*

Don't get me wrong, I'm not a kill-joy.
But did you ever spend four hours
using a shovel, a pick
and everything short of dynamite
to clear the sidewalk of ice and snow
so that little old ladies
can waddle to the store for parakeet seed
and so I. Magnin's and Bonwit Teller's Christmas catalogues
could be delivered to each consumer
and so the hoodlums wouldn't fall and fracture
their necks as they break into somebody's house;
and go to bed with a pain in yer back
like nobody's business
and blisters on yer hands
and wake up the next morning
to look out at three feet of snow on the sidewalk?

54

# Dubuffet's *Winter Garden*

Bring a hat, mittens and scarf
if you plan to stay for more than five minutes.
Frostbite can be painful.
Anyone not wishing to visit winter
should proceed to the Impressionists:
if you can't stand the cold
get out of the igloo.
As you sit on a snowbank
gazing at the permafrost
listen carefully and you will hear
the wind plotting a blizzard.
You will notice the tracks and footprints
of trappers with huskies, polar bears,
arctic wolves and snow leopards.
None of these will disturb your visit
to the winter garden – normally;
they're only allowed in after closing.
Let's step into the second chamber.
Your sandal has disappeared in the snow?
Your mini-skirt is frozen solid?
Your walrus moustache is dripping icicles?
What do you expect when you come dressed for Tahiti?
Your nose is red, your teeth are chattering,
I suggest you join your friends
in front of that Gauguin.

# Winter
*(after Sei Shonagon)*


I. *Empress Sadako Considers Snow*

When I wore my hair
straight across my forehead,
I loved deep drifts
in my father's yard.
We would spend all day
making a snow mountain,
praying to Goddess Shirayama
not to let it melt.
Now I stir the red embers
in my brazier, watching flurries
through the icy lattice
and have ordered that no one
disturb the snow outside my rooms
by shuffling wooden clogs there
or heaping it into a silly mountain.
Snow is shapeliest when left alone.


II. *Silver*

I'm the only one who seems to care anymore
about the Winter Festival at Kamo.
The evening should be cold enough for snow,
with bonfires, dancers and musicians.
First I hear the sound of drums,
then my eyes follow the light
from the flaming pine torches.
I am always overjoyed at the costumes
of lustrous silk, frozen stiff with ice
and the palace roof outlined in white
seems thatched in silver.
Everyone says, 'You get too excited.'
How can I help it?
I will stay up remembering
until the dawn bell.


56

### III. *Men and Precipitation*

My dislike of rain is profound.
Your hair goes stringy,
mud cakes your shoes and hem
and the whole world
becomes a drippy damp
annoyingly stupid place.
But if a man arrives during a storm,
dressed in the yellow-green
of a Chamberlain
or, best of all, in a proper Court robe
moistened by sleet,
I can't hide my admiration.
I forget all about the hateful showers,
organise dry clothes, a warm drink
and pay careful attention
to wringing out his costume.
Nothing pleases me more
than a secret meeting
with a man covered in raindrops.

# Look No Further

You can do anything in this room.
If you sit at this beech table
surveying the pine ceiling
with a plum in your mouth,
you could be royalty.
Up above the skylight
pine cones and wood pigeons are
sheltering me from the world.
A woven African basket
is stuffed like the horn of plenty.
A sink dispenses the source of life.
Cabinets with supplies
will treat your slightest stomach rumble.
A room of dreams:
What would you like to do?
Watch TV? Knit a sweater?
Listen to the radio? Eat an ice-cube?
Cook a dinner? Read the paper?
It's all here – look no further.

# In the Garden of Earthly Delights
*(for Nuala and John)*


I lean back into a flowery cushion
to see a rosebud creeping skyward behind my head.
The breeze, a wafting violin,
serenades your dancing sun-umbrella.
A sparrow tweets so much
it has to wet its whistle
at the stone bird-bath.
A crunchy strawberry thing melts on my tongue,
globs of cream beckon my finger.
A carefree day sipping wine,
a row of geraniums on the windowsill humming.
A shy mezzo-soprano opens a window –
or is she singing through the crack
where the french doors are twinkling?
She looks around, anyway,
from her hide-out and decides on Mahler.
How did you train the bees on your foliage
to do those dexterous little tricks?
I want to put all this stuff
into a bottle and display it like a ship.

# Bye

This is today –
the day I will wave at you
from a bus
a departure lounge
a moving car
a doorway.
It is more civilised
than sobbing
or hysterics –
no gnarly scenes
of naked sorrow
are called for.
Put your hand up
decide if you want
finger twiddles
or arm activity.
Either way
keep up the momentum.
Don't remember anything
you meant to say or do.
Keep distance your goal.
All of us could think up
wonderful excuses
for staying
where we are.
That's why we invented
the hand-flap
and the easy-to-lip-read
'Bye'.

# Remind Me

I said – listen to me carefully –
you have crossed the Rocky Mountains
on a plane full of Indonesian immigrants.
You landed at Los Angeles
and saw tall palm trees
and then flew north to San Francisco
so don't play innocent.
You were met at the airport
and used the walk-a-lator to view
the exhibition of Mexican skeleton art.
I kept pleading with you to focus
what attention you could possibly muster
on the Chinese food in front of you.
The metaphorical drive over that
Golden Gate Bridge was beyond
your capacity to grasp.
You do recall the back and forth
hither and thither road to Bolinas
and how it was dark in the mountains – don't you?
The car veered either right or left
onto a gravel lane and then
you stumbled up the porch steps.
Does any of this ring a bell?
There was a ladder with carpet-covered rungs
up to the sleeping area.
Say you remember that much!

*We were driving to a new mall*
*in third gear in a Volkswagen camper –*
*and I kept telling my sister*
*to shift into fourth.*
*I stood staring at the latest technology*
*in toothbrushes, home alarms,*
*talking car accessories, personal organisers.*
*At another town a Danish butcher*
*told us how to successfully barbeque a salmon.*
*We chewed corn chips while travelling.*
The Joy of Cooking *was propped open*
*to page 621: Marble Angel Cake.*

*A red hummingbird in a hand.*
*I left the station wagon and threw up*
*facing a peeled trunk of eucalyptus.*
*Someone had dropped his trousers*
*outside the dry cleaners in Mill Valley.*
*Burn-outs lounged in the parks in Berkeley.*
*You could hear blow-outs*
*from the children of the burn-outs*
*through the clearing behind the bushes.*
*People were swimming in a volcanic lake.*
*Buddhist monks farmed under a cliff.*
*What was it again that you loved*
*in the antique clothes shop in Olema?*
*I couldn't explain the outside world to you,*
*it was too far away*
*and didn't sell frozen yogurt.*

I tried again to remind her – what about the man
at the foster home – didn't he ask you
how to spell Bhopal
while he sat at his word-processor?
You must have gone out the kitchen door
at some stage to pick mulberries for a pie
because you had purple hands
and red scratches after that.
It smelled like a dream baking.
Does it seem any clearer?
What you need to find
is the silky tassle pull of that time.
Once you have it in your fist
you can recover it back from nowhere.
The kitchen was where you left from.
Trace over the road to Dogtown
past the church, the lagoon, the organic farmer.

It is on your planet –
you could get there right now if you tried.
The fake New England houses
built for nostalgic Californians
on Skywalker Ranch
are somebody's hang-up.
You could go out
and invent some hang-ups
of your own.

# Hanging Out in Dogtown

The rope hammock
rocks in the wind
between tree and roof.
Below on the wooden porch
ordinary things go on:
a yellow bird lands and departs,
a jade plant gets a tan.
Under my elbow and foot
wild plants, saplings,
vines, hidden creatures
cushion the air I swing in
with heavy soft green.
The Appaloosas are munching,
the metal wind-mill is creaking,
the hills are scorching.
Pushing against the porch railing
daintily with my toe,
I increase my swaying speed
until this magical flying contraption
appears as clear, weightless
and as graceful as this
summer afternoon
in Dogtown of my dreams.

## First Visit to Their Daughter

You will see
who I am
pretty soon.
I do not know yet
if you will like
my plates
or the carpet
or how I lead my life
such as it is.
It will be a surprise
to us all.
First I will open the door
and everyone
will put down their luggage.
Now at this stage
what are your
immediate impressions?
Have I fulfilled expectations
or are you disappointed
at the curtains?
I will be pretending
not to care
while watching your reaction
to whether I was
worth it or not.

# La Toilette

The slimy wind was pushing into my face.
I witnessed snakes and fireballs
plopping out of people's mouths.
A diseased rat wound its tail
around my ankle
on a dreary Dublin sidewalk.
October was lurking everywhere.
I think: if I can just make it
as far as the bathtub,
I might survive this awful day.
Now inside a cozy room,
I wade into a pond of steaming water
and disturb a flamingo
preening her feathers.
An angel fish
is blowing bubbles at my feet.

II

Let me see.
The directions say
to keep the conditioner
on your hair
for fifteen minutes.
After my bath
I will take a shower
to rinse my hair.
It will be a long bath
and a leisurely shower.
Then of course
the *après-bain*
will use up no less
than another half hour
when I can invent
further endless alibis
for basking here.

III

Stepping softly from the bath,
I reach for my radiator-heated kimono
and press the handiest little switch
over the mirror to view my teeth.
All during the above,
a thick, steadfast towel
has been absorbing the excess moisture
from my pink feet.
Then I goof around with my hair,
arranging it in elaborate piles,
yawn luxuriously
and head for bed.

# Dumbarton Oaks Library

I say good morning to the museum guard.
He slams the heavy door closed behind me
and announces that the magnolias are in bloom today.
I am in the glass-roofed passageway
but I call over my shoulder,
'Really? I must have a look at them.'
Beside me in a display case,
pre-Columbian turquoise bead
is resting in two tiny brass hands.
Four marble steps lead into the breezy corridor.
I creak past the ballroom and sitting-room
with drapes flapping their arms at me.
Inside the stuffy wooden office upstairs,
I move a pile of catalogue cards,
re-arrange stacks of books,
give the table a shove
and open the huge window.
Outside in the formal gardens,
two men are looking for a contact lens
lost in the flower beds.
I lean over the windowsill thinking
*so that's a magnolia.*

# The Great Blasket Island

Six men born on this island
have come back after twenty-one years.
They climb up the overgrown roads
to their family houses
and come out shaking their heads.
The roofs have fallen in
and birds have nested in the rafters.
All the white-washed rooms
all the nagging and praying
and scolding and giggling
and crying and gossiping
are scattered in the memories of these men.
One says, 'Ten of us, blown to the winds –
some in England, some in America, some in Dublin.
Our whole way of life – extinct.'
He blinks back the tears
and looks across the island
past the ruined houses, the cliffs
and out to the horizon.

Listen, mister, most of us cry sooner or later
over a Great Blasket Island of our own.

# The Sounds of Earth

*(broadcast from Voyager-II to the universe)*

Here is the most popular sound first:
we call it talking – it is also known fondly as
shooting off one's mouth, discussing,
chewing the fat, yammering, blabbing,
conversing, confiding, debating, speaking,
gossiping, hollering and yakking.
So here's a whole bunch of jaw creakers.
How come none of you guys out there
don't yap at us – we'd sure like to hear
what you have to say
on the subject of where the hell you are.

For our second selection,
we will now play a medley of music
which you may or may not care for
since as I know myself
music is a very personal thing.
Why not aim a little musical extravaganza earthward?
As I say – we're waiting.

Now for our something-for-everyone finale.
Here's a rush hour traffic jam,
brakes are screeching – horns are blasting.
This is the phone ringing with typewriters
and computer printers in the background.
I'm very partial to this next one:
a rocking chair creaking on a porch
with birds and crickets chirping.
To finish up, we've got a lawn mower,
knitting needles, a hammer, a saw,
a football stadium after a score,
a door shutting, a baby crying
and a kitchen sink filling with water
for a cosmic thigh-slapper.

We're equal opportunity down here
so if you're a blob or have three heads
or look like something the cat dragged in –
we won't bat an eyelid.

## Swivel Shelf

Not only is it impossible
to stay inside tonight
but it is equally impossible
to go anywhere.
That's when the cabinets
in the kitchen come into their own.
It is the open and close
look up look down
move the can of soup over to the left
and stack the box of lasagne
on top of the box of rice game.
You know how you hate a
pub's smoky atmosphere:
thank your fate
for producing cabinets
with a swivel shelf
so you can enjoy taking stock
of the non-perishables
without that upsetting position
where you kneel down,
open the door
and insert your head fully.

# Getting through the Night

### I

We part ways for the night.
I slip inside a dream bag
and zip it up when the last toe
is losing consciousness for another day.
If you didn't turn on the light at eight,
who knows how long I'd sleep?
Your nightime path is strewn
with misery and corpses,
or poets soberly discussing
literary points in calf-bound rooms.
Sometimes I can hear you
pounding on the ceiling of my dreams
for me to turn the noise down.

### II

I was upstairs in a loft
or on one of those sleeping devices
that are always being invented
on Judson Avenue.
Maybe I was copying out
a poem onto the wall
we use for poetic graffiti.
Maybe I was only reading
when I heard you calling
'Julie, Julie' from downstairs.
'WHAT?' I screamed
so loudly that I woke myself up
three thousand miles and fifteen years away.

## Leaving Home

The first night
you'll lie face-down and cry.
That helps to clear your head.
In the morning, you aren't sure
what to do about breakfast
since you're in a strange house.
You unfold the map
your father gave you
and follow the mark
of his felt-tip pen
along outlines of streets
that seemed impossible
to imagine last week
but now stalk right outside.

# I Don't Ask Myself

what I'm doing snoozing in a bed
in a pitch black room
in a house enveloped
in misty fog on fields
located in the middle of nowheresville
somewhere on an island
out floating in tons of $H_2O$.
The end result might
overload my fuses.
I merely stick my nose
out from under the puffy quilt
and listen closely
to the intercontinental jet overhead
and imagine the passengers
slumped in seats
mouths hanging open
trying to catch a few winks
before they encounter loved ones
on the far side of the planet.

## Saturday Afternoon in Dublin

Dietrich Fischer-Dieskau is in the process
of depressing me singing
the 'Der Einsame im Herbst' section
of *Das Lied von der Erde*.
A flute is playing as I look
at my sisters photographed in New York
in a crowd of twenty-five thousand people
getting ready for a bicycle tour.
I meet them for a few days
every two years or so
but I don't know them anymore;
only how they used to be
before I went away.
Are you crying yet?
Sometimes you get to know your relatives
better when they're pinned down
like butterfly specimens
wearing baseball cap and crash helmet respectively.
Kate, I see, has a blue-faced watch
with snappy red band.
Ellen has let her hair grow.
They both smile nervously
because my father is taking the picture
in the middle of the throng.
Dietrich, meanwhile, has moved on to a beautiful, sad,
song with harps – I'm glad I don't know any German –
it's even sadder hearing words sung
that make no sense.
He says, 'Ja, ja' better than anyone.
It isn't music for New York, really.
A Hopper etching: 'Night Shadows',
an afternoon in Dublin looking
out the arid window for inspiration,
wanting so many things to happen –
that's when it gets to you.
Are you crying yet?

# Moon Message

I was following the dancing ball
of the moon until it hopped
into a cloud and hid.
Someone in my vicinity
was smoking in the No-Smoking car.
I'm surrounded by Irish people
and a lady nagging at her kid,
'Patrick, come on, we're getting off the train.'
I can't blame the Irish
for travelling on a train
in their own country –
it just surprises me
to be in such a foreign location.
Me and my Maxwell House paper cup
seem to be the only Yankee products
roaming to Limerick
through the peat smoke and bushes.
I like to think of the moon as a Yank.
He saw me looking out a car window
in 1967 coasting down the outer-drive
beside Lake Michigan.
I whispered something to him.
Tonight, for the first time
in almost twenty years
I can hear him answer back.

# Café – Dempster Avenue

if you sit in the café
surrounded by
raw brick
raw wood
and folk music
the man
at the next table
will talk to you
and you
should talk back
or else
don't come
and read the paper
in the café
expecting coffee
and banana bread
that isn't
the point
at all

# Misty Island

Sei Shonagon's *Pillow Book* tells
how the smell of pine torches
wafts through the air
and gets into your carriage
when you're travelling through the dark
in a procession someplace.
Here on this island in the fog,
I'll have to take her word – 'delightful' – for it.
As I read the part where she says
'is wafted through the air and pervades
the carriage in which one is travelling',
'Down by the Salley Gardens' starts playing on the radio.

**Julie O'Callaghan** was born in Chicago in 1954. She came to live in Ireland in 1974 and now works part-time in the library of Trinity College, Dublin. Her first book, *Edible Anecdotes* (Dolmen Press), was a Poetry Book Society Recommendation. Her second collection, *What's What* (Bloodaxe, 1991), is a Poetry Book Society Choice.

Her poems have appeared in major UK and Irish publications and are represented in many anthologies, including *Firebird 4* (Penguin), *Soho Square* (Bloomsbury), *The New Younger Irish Poets* (Blackstaff) and *Is That the New Moon?* (Collins).

Her children's poems were published in *Bright Lights Blaze Out* (1986) in the Oxford University Press Three Poets series, and her first book of poems for children, *Taking My Pen for a Walk* was published by Orchard Books in 1988.

She has given many poetry readings at festivals and in schools as well as on radio and television. The Irish Arts Council awarded her literary bursaries in 1985 and 1990.